What's in this book

This book belongs to

_____

我比你高 I am taller than you

学习内容 Contents

沟通 Communication

描述他人体格外貌
Describe someone's physical appearance

比较身高
Compare heights

生词 New words

★	高	tall
★	矮	short
★	个子	height
★	脸	face
★	圆	round
★	方	square
★	比	than
	哥哥	elder brother
	肚子	belly
	好看	good-looking

150
120
0
60
30

背景介绍：
浩浩、伊森和艾文在比谁的个子高。

我比你高。你比我矮。

I am taller than you. You are shorter than me.

跨学科学习 Project

了解并计算体重指数

Learn about the body mass
index (BMI) and calculate it

文化 Cultures

历史上伟大的人物

Great people in history

参考答案：
1 I am 1.20 metres tall./I am 123 centimetres tall.
2 David is the tallest student in my class./I don't know who is the tallest student.
3 I think Ivan is taller./Ethan is as tall as Ivan.

Get ready

1 How tall are you?

2 Who is the tallest student in your class?

3 Who is taller, Ethan or Ivan?

读一读 Read

故事大意：
伊森和艾文在比谁高，浩浩帮他们量身高。艾文问浩浩是否比他们矮，浩浩开玩笑说自己比他们好看。

事物间进行比较、对比时，我们用"比"肯定句式为"A比B+比较结果"，如"艾 比伊森高。"否定句式为"A没有/不如比较结果"，如"艾文没有/不如伊森高。

bǐ
比

gē ge
哥哥

gāo
高

ǎi
矮

"高"和"矮" 一对反义词

参考问题和答案：
1 What are Ivan and Ethan doing? (They are comparing their heights.)
2 Why does Ivan look so excited? (Because he thinks he is taller than his elder brother.)

"哥哥，我比你高，你比我矮。"艾文说。

gè zi

个子

"你们的个子一样高。"
浩浩说。

参考问题和答案：

1 What is Hao Hao doing? (He is measuring Ethan's and Ivan's heights.)
2 Who is taller, Ivan or Ethan? How tall are they? (They all have the same height. They are all 1.20 metres tall.)

5

liǎn
脸

"方"和"圆"是一对反义词。

fāng
方

yuán
圆

"伊森的脸方，艾文的脸圆。"浩浩又说。

参考问题和答案：
What are Ivan and Ethan doing?
(Ivan is measuring Hao Hao's height.
Ethan is helping Hao Hao to see his
height in the mirror.)
Is Hao Hao as tall as the twin
brothers? (No, he is slightly shorter.)

"浩浩，你看我们比你
高多少呢？"艾文问。

参考问题和答案：

1. What is Hao Hao doing with the mirror? (He is looking at himself in the mirror.)
2. Does Hao Hao feel satisfied with his look in the mirror? (He is happy with his look and he thinks he is better-looking than the twin brothers.)

hǎo kàn
好看

"你们比我高，但我比你们好看！"浩浩说。

参考问题和答案：
Why do the boys laugh so heartily? (They are joking that Hao Hao's face and belly are both round.)

dù zi
肚子

"是啊，浩浩的脸圆，肚子也圆。"艾文说。

Let's think

1 Recall the story. Put a tick or a cross. 提醒学生回忆故事，观察第4至7页。

2 How tall are you? Draw below. 让学生回忆最近一次量的身高，学生也可以互相量，然后在自己的年龄处画上相应的身高。

询问他人身高时，我们说"你多高？"。

你多高？

New words

1 Learn the new words.

延伸活动：
学生两人一组，互相比一比身高和脸型，然后用完整的中文句子表达出来。
建议句式："我（的个子）比你……""你的脸……"

好看
比 个子
高
矮
方
脸
哥哥
肚子
圆

2 Look and complete the sentences. Write the letters.

a 比　b 圆　c 高　d 矮　e 脸　f 个子

1 他___f___高，___e___方。

2 她脸___b___，个子不___c___。

3 她___a___他___d___。

待学生完成练习后，老师总结"比"字句的重点在于"比"前面的
事物，从而相应地确定比较的结果。

听听说说 Listen and say

第一题录音稿：
1 他和哥哥一样高，浩浩比他矮，他是谁？
2 他个子不高，他的肚子圆脸也圆，他是谁？
3 他的个子高高的，脸方方的，他很好看。

🎧 03 **1** Listen and circle the correct pictures.

🎧 04 **2** Look at the pictures. Listen to the sto

1

2

3

①

矮个子在前面，高个子在后面。

③

你们圆圆的脸，比红苹果好看。

12

第二题参考问题与答案：

1 How does Ms Wu position the students to take the group picture? (She asks the taller students to stand at the back and the shorter ones at the front.)
2 Do you like taking pictures together with your schoolmates? (Yes, I do. Because it is fun and I like to keep good memories./I don't mind.)

nd say.

鼓励学生尽可能多角度地表达图画中的信息，同时，一种意思可以用多种方式表达。如"尺子爸爸比笔妈妈高。"和"笔妈妈比尺子爸爸矮。"

3 Talk about the stationery family with your friend. Use these words.

比　高　矮　圆

方　脸　个子

尺子爸爸……

笔妈妈……

本子哥哥……

橡皮妹妹……

Task

Find out who the two tallest boys and girls are in your class.
Draw and say.
先让学生目测判断哪几个同学是班里比较高的，然后进一步量身高确定最高的男生和女生各两位，最后把结果在图表上表示出来，并说一说。
建议句式："……是最高的。""……比……高。"

你多高？
谁比谁高？

……

cm
180
170
160
150
140
130
120

（名字）＿＿＿＿　＿＿＿＿　＿＿＿＿　＿＿＿＿

Game

本题旨在练习"A 比 B+ 比较结果"句式，左侧一列即 A，中间列即 B，右侧一列即比较结果。
老师任意说出左侧一列中的词，学生参考该词同一行的其他词来说出完整的句子。如：老师说"这个苹果"，学生则说"这个苹果比那个苹果大。"

Listen to your teacher and help Hao Hao complete the sentences.

这个苹果
……

这个苹果比那个苹果大。

这个苹果	那个苹果	大
蛋糕	糖果	好吃
果汁	茶	好喝
红本子	蓝本子	好看
姐姐	我	高
弟弟	哥哥	矮
男孩	女孩	多
橡皮	铅笔	少

Song

"高不高""圆不圆"是想对具体情况做确认的一种问法，即"X不X"。也可以说"X吗"。回答时说"X"或"不X"。

🎧 05 Listen and sing.

你的个子高不高？

她的脸儿圆不圆？

我们比一比。

你的个子高，

她的脸儿圆，

我的肚子大，

大家不一样，

大家都好看。

课堂用语 Classroom language

我忘记了。
I forgot.

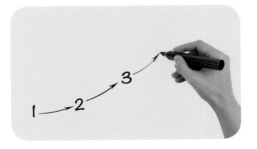

接下来，……
Next, ...

1 Learn and trace the stroke. 老师示范笔画动作，学生跟着做：用手在空中画出"竖提"。

竖提

2 Learn the components. Colour 比 red and 高 green in the characters.

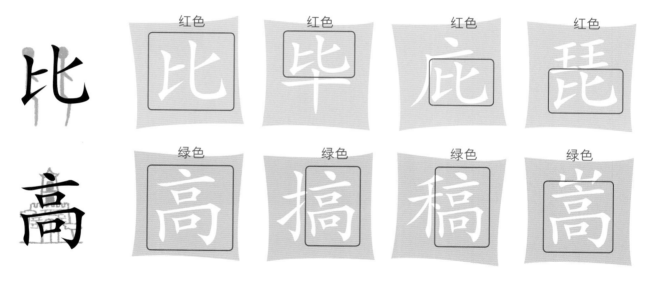

比

红色 比   红色 毕   红色 庇   红色 琵

高

绿色 高   绿色 搞   绿色 稿   绿色 嵩

3 Look at the words carefully. Tick the correct sentences.

提醒学生注意"比"与"高"的正确写法，与错别字作区分。并让学生说说错别字哪里错了。

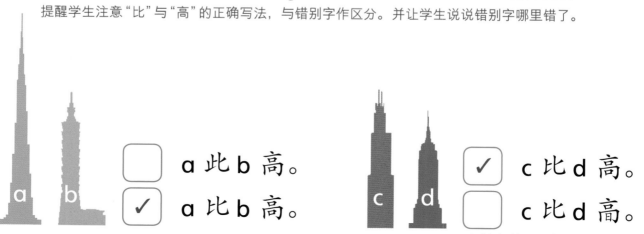

☐ a 此 b 高。

☑ a 比 b 高。

☑ c 比 d 高。

☐ c 比 d 高。

向学生说明汉字中不存在"高"字，它是电脑合成的。

4 Trace and write the characters.

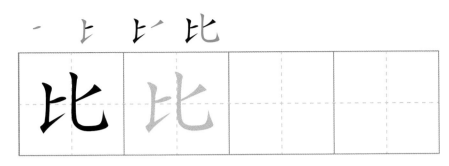

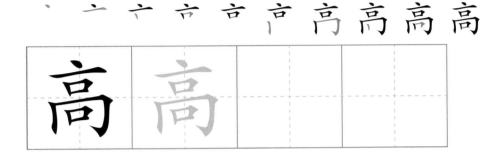

5 Write and say.

 我 比 哥哥矮。  我 比 妹妹 高。

汉字小常识 Did you know?

Colour the component that encloses another component red.

这些字的结构是（左三）包围结构。

Some characters include a component which encloses another component on three sides — left, right and bottom.

多元学习 Connections

1 Statues are built to honour great people in history. Match the names to the photos. Write the letters.

a Abraham Lincoln

b Aristotle

c Genghis Khan

d Napoleon

e Queen Victoria

老师可简单介绍图片中的人物：
a 林肯是美国历史上最伟大的总统之一。
b 亚里士多德是古希腊哲学家。
c 成吉思汗是中国古代杰出的政治家、军事家。
d 拿破仑是法国军事家、政治家与法学家。
e 维多利亚女王是在位第二长的英国君主。

2 Find out about a great man or woman in your country. Complete the table and tell your friend about him/her.

Paste a photo here

国家：＿＿＿＿＿   名字：＿＿＿＿＿

他/她叫 ＿＿＿＿＿＿＿＿＿＿。

他/她的个子 ＿＿＿＿＿＿＿＿。

他/她的脸 ＿＿＿＿＿＿＿＿＿。

老师让学生上网搜索伟人的相关信息，将照片下载后贴在左侧，完成表格后与同学交流。

Project

身体质量指数（BMI）是一个衡量人体胖瘦程度以及是否健康的标准。以世界卫生组织的国际标准，当指数为 18.5～25 时，体重一般为正常，指数过小则体重过轻，过大则为肥胖。但对于成长发育中的儿童，应结合当地相关统计数据来看。

1 Have you heard of the body mass index (BMI)? Find out how it works and talk about it.

BMI shows us whether we are overweight or underweight in relation to our height.

$$BMI = \frac{weight\ (kg)}{height\ (metre)\ \times\ height\ (metre)}$$

你的 BMI 是多少？

15.2

我的 BMI 是……，比你的 BMI 高吗？

21.0

18.8

 Your BMI

Your weight: _____ kg
Your height: _____ m
Result (kg/m²): _____

17.9

各地区的 BMI 标准不同。如亚洲标准中，指数 18.5～22.9 为正常，欧美人种的指数在 18.5～24.9 为正常。

2 Different countries sometimes have different BMI standards. Find out the standards in your country and compare your BMI with them.

我的 BMI

温习 Checkpoint

从大树底部开始，从下到上依次完成练习，最后帮助猫咪到达树的顶端。

1 Help the cat get to the top of the tree.

Draw a 圆脸.

你的个子高吗？
Answer in Chinese.

我的个子（很）高。/我的个子
不高。/我的个子很矮。

Compare your height with one of your friends' and say 我比你……

我比你高/矮。

Say the opposite of
高 in Chinese.

矮

How to say 'tall'
in Chinese?

高

我 比 它们 高。

评核方法：
学生两人一组，互相考察评价表内单词和句子的听说读写。交际沟通部分由老师朗读要求，
学生再互相对话。如果达到了某项技能要求，则用色笔将星星或小辣椒涂色。

2 Work with your friend. Colour the stars and the chillies.

Words	说	读	写
高	☆	☆	☆
矮	☆	☆	🌶
个子	☆	☆	🌶
脸	☆	☆	🌶
圆	☆	☆	🌶
方	☆	☆	🌶
比	☆	☆	☆
哥哥	☆	🌶	🌶
肚子	☆	🌶	🌶
好看	☆	🌶	🌶

Sentences	说	读	写
他的脸圆，肚子也圆。	☆	🌶	🌶
我比你高，你比我矮。	☆	☆	🌶

Describe someone's physical appearance	☆
Compare heights	☆

3 What does your teacher say?

评核建议：
根据学生课堂表现，分别给予"太棒了！(Excellent!)"、
"不错！(Good!)"或"继续努力！(Work harder!)"的评价，
再让学生圈出左侧对应的表情，以记录自己的学习情况。

My teacher says ...

Words I remember

高	gāo	tall
矮	ǎi	short
个子	gè zi	height
脸	liǎn	face
圆	yuán	round
方	fāng	square
比	bǐ	than
哥哥	gē ge	elder brother
肚子	dù zi	belly
好看	hǎo kàn	good-looking

延伸活动：
1 学生用手遮盖英文，读中文单词，并思考单词意思；
2 学生用手遮盖中文单词，看着英文说出对应的中文单词；
3 学生三人一组，尽量运用中文单词分角色复述故事。

Other words

一样	yī yàng	same
又	yòu	again
但	dàn	but
啊	a	(used at the end of a sentence to express agreement)

OXFORD
UNIVERSITY PRESS

Oxford University Press is a department of the University of Oxford.
It furthers the University's objective of excellence in research, scholarship,
and education by publishing worldwide. Oxford is a registered trade mark of
Oxford University Press in the UK and in certain other countries

Published in Hong Kong by
Oxford University Press (China) Limited
39th Floor, One Kowloon, 1 Wang Yuen Street, Kowloon Bay,
Hong Kong

Illustrated by Anne Lee, KK Ng, KY Chan and Wildman

Photographs for reproduction permitted by Dreamstime.com

China National Publications Import & Export (Group) Corporation is an authorized distributor of
Oxford Elementary Chinese.

Please contact content@cnpiec.com.cn or 86-10-65856782

ISBN: 978-0-19-082198-2

10 9 8 7 6 5 4 3 2

Teacher's Edition
ISBN: 978-0-19-082210-1

10 9 8 7 6 5 4 3 2